# SWEAR WORD COLORING BOOK

**I Don't Give A Damn Adult Coloring Book**
**Featuring Sweary Words & Funny Phrases**

Rainbow Coloring & Joe Ellison

Follow us on Facebook: **Rainbow Coloring Books**
Add me on my personal FB: **Joe Ellison (http://bit.ly/1r31Bay)**
Instagram : **Rainbowcoloring**
or add us on Snapchat: **Rainbowcoloring**

Get free pages to enjoy and color, bonuses, discounts and a behind the scenes look at our process.

**DO YOU WANT TO WIN A FREE COPY OF OUR UPCOMING BOOKS?**

Contact us at **Joe.rainbowcoloring@gmail.com** or on **Snapchat/Facebook/Instagram**, send us « How can I get a free copy ? » and we will explain you how you can win a free copy of our upcoming books ☺

**DOWNLOAD THE DIGITAL PDF EDITION OF THIS BOOK FOR UNLIMITED PRINTING**

http://bit.ly/1WtVcSM

**REVIEWS ARE OUR OXYGEN AND HELPS US CREATE AWESOME BOOKS. WOULD YOU BE KIND ENOUGH TO LEAVE US A REVIEW ON AMAZON?**

THE TRUTH IS THAT MY LIFE IS NOT GOING...

52920595R00035

Made in the USA
San Bernardino, CA
01 September 2017